Fellowship of Extraordinary Women
September 2018
Ministry Teaching and Journal

Kimberly Joy Krueger

This work is based on the experiences of individuals. Every effort has been made to ensure the accuracy of the content. For permission requests, write to the publisher addressed,

"Attention: Permissions Coordinator," at the address below:

FEW International Publications
P.O. Box 271
Mukwonago, WI 53149

ISBN-13: 978-1-949494-04-4

A Women's Forum:
Emotional Resilience

Prayer To Start

Thank you, God . . .

"For this morning, for these women, and for the idea that we *can be* emotionally resilient. You glory in that and we glory you in that. You give us hope that we don't have to be crushed and broken. You take our low moments and take us higher with you. I pray we walk out of here with one solid thing to do to be emotionally resilient. Amen."

*"You need self-control
in an out-of-control world."*
Jack C. Collins

*"You can have faith, but if it's not connected
to hope in a way that is not positive
expectation, you have to change your mind
set on that. Faith should be connected to
positive hope."*
Joyce Meyer

*"We are afflicted in every way, but not
crushed; perplexed, but not driven to despair;
persecuted, but not forsaken; struck down, but
not destroyed; always carrying in the body
the death of Jesus, so that the life of Jesus may
also be manifested in our bodies."*

2 Corinthians 4:8
When was the last time you cried and why?

If I burst into tears while talking about emotional resilience, I've learned that's just God's test for me. If I'm talking about anger, I'm ticked off for thirty days. As I create this, I'm emotional. And, if I'm honest, I like to see people cry when I teach. Not because I want them to be hurt, but I want them to be moved.

We are afflicted in every way, but not crushed; perplexed, but not driven to despair; persecuted, but not forsaken; struck down, but not destroyed; always carrying in the body the death of Jesus, so that the life of Jesus may also be manifested in our bodies.

It takes resilience to say that and even more to live that. Paul wrote that and believers were essentially waiting persecution and then imminent death. If he can say that, facing death, can't we say it facing life? Not to minimize the pressures of life, which are real and big, being a woman this day in age, but, as the Jack Collins quote says, we need self-control in an out-of-control world.

The Message . . .

"Business Strategy" You hear that phrase all the time. Business experts have much to say about the importance of strategy in building a successful business.

For a long time my own out-of-control world served to bring me down. Just like any sickness *under* the surface, it has to *come to* the surface to be dealt with . God *allowed* my lack to be brought to the surface. All of my natural emotional propensities were brought to the forefront: as a child, teen, and mother of many, I struggled with unforgiveness and anger.

I was choosing anger because it was safer than pain. The way I handled it was more destructive than pain, itself. I had to get control *of me*. I was trying to control everybody else, too. . . the rebellions from being rebellious, the stressed from being stressed, the sad from being sad. That's a hard way to live.

I sat in counselor's office one day, and was told: "You have a prob. Your problem is identifying whose problem the problem is."

So I reassigned problems. You know how you assign things to people? Well, in my mind, I put post-its on all of the problems in my world. Only one problem had my name on it . . . me.

Other people's feelings, mistakes, and messes did not have a post-it with my name on it. I only had to address me.

Now, when someone brings a problem to me, I listen to my internal response. Is it *'Oh great, what am I going to do?'* or *'Bummer. What are you going to do?'*

It's still empathy, but I was free from "fixing" and they were free to deal. It took growing pains and it's painful to grow from difficulty.

God says, "You're growing."

"I don't like it," I say back.

"You will like it," He reassures.

It's like breaking down muscle; you have to break it down to build it up.

I learned to own *me*. My emotions were on me. No more thinking, *'You make me so . . . . mad, sad, frustrated, etc.'* OWN the emotions.

If we can say to someone, "you make me so mad," why do we not say, "you make me so peaceful, content, joyful?" It's because it's a choice. If positive emotions are a choice, so are anger, resentment . . . and losing it!

Emotions are powerful and strong and we DO have a choice.

Rely on truth.

Rely on new tools.

That changes how we respond emotionally. You're better off waiting until you have clarity.

~~~~

How many times are we **acting on those negative emotions**? I began to say, instead of going negative, "I'm not sure what I'm going to do about this," and I'd give myself . . . *time*. It's one of the greatest gifts I gave myself.

We often **match negative emotions**. (*'I'm angry because you're angry.'*) Why don't we do this for happy emotions?

Sometimes, we have **(negative) emotional waves**, when we wake up under a cloud, and only a happy event would break us out of it. Joyce Meyer calls this, "emotional foreboding."

I lived in a storm of waves and wind and thunder and lightning. We must learn to anchor. The storms still come, but the anchor is truth and self-control. It's a practice. You need to practice . . . get better, get more flexible, add more approaches.

Get better at *controlling* anger, discouragement, and frustration.

One of the biggest breakthroughs I had was when I learned I *had* self-control.

"I can't help it," was my mantra. I believed that. It was a lie. I heard a sermon say, "The fruit of the spirit is self-control" and that means *it's already deposited in you*.

I'm continuing to increase my belief that I HAVE self-control If Jesus lives in you, you HAVE it, too!

The thing we need most for emotional resilience is self-control!

Self-control is WAY underestimated in terms of its importance in our lives and way undervalued in our lives. Do we just accept that part of who we are is self-control? If we do that, are we denying the process of sanctification? He came to save all of us . . . shouldn't there be some progress in the area of self-control?

God is telling us that we can progress emotionally in our lives.

WHY is it so important that we become more emotionally resilient in our lives?

It's about leadership in faith, family, and business. That's where people are watching us. Don't you think emotional resilience is part of what they see when they watch us?

Emotional Resilience refers to one's ability to adapt to stressful situations or crises. More resilient people are able to "roll with the punches" and adapt to adversity without lasting difficulties; less resilient people have a harder time with stress and life changes, both major and minor.

Emotional Competence is described as the essential social skills to recognize, interpret, and respond constructively to emotions in yourself and others.

It's basically emotional intelligence. Recognize, interpret, and respond constructively to emotions. Is this the first time you've thought about emotional resilience in terms of your leadership?

Forum Q1: How important do you deem emotional resilience (We'll call it ER, but it's also known as emotional competence) to be in faith, family and business...and why?

_____

_____

_____

_____

From the Forum . . .

I was so glad to see this topic because I need better ER skills than fight, flight, or freeze. People need me. I can't just not be there for my family, for my business.

The importance of ER to our leadership is a 10 on a scale of 1 to 10!

It's okay to allow emotion if that emotion is *productive*. We're human.

With faith, family, and business, use it as a temperature gage. Evaluate what your emotion should be. You sometimes need to make a conscious effort to SHOW emotions, too, so you don't come across as cold or callous.

Emotions come out differently in faith, family or home, and business. ER in faith increases when we go through and overcome a challenge. The testimony of that helps to increase the ER of others, too!

ER Is really having faith in God. Courage to give it to Him. In family, I turn to prayer. If we are going at it, we pray and it's immediately taken away. In business, love the client where they are at. Take yourself out of it and take them where they are. They aren't in the same place as me. I need to take them there.

Everything about ER should be consistent whether in faith, family, or business. As team leader, as Mom, in ministry, we need to set the tone we want from others. Sometimes it doesn't always feel calm, bold, or courageous. And those days take intentionality. Be consistent so they see the same person everywhere.

Strategic prayer tip – make your prayer into a phone screen saver! Remember to pray that!

From the Word . . .

"Put up with each other. Forgive the things you are holding against one another. Forgive, just as the Lord forgave you."

~Colossians 3:13

"Don't pay back evil with evil. Be careful to do what everyone thinks is right. If possible, live in peace with everyone. Do that as much as you can. My friends, don't

try to get even. Leave room for God to show his anger. It is written, 'I am the One who judges people. I will pay them back,' (Deuteronomy 32:35) says the Lord. Do just the opposite. Scripture says, 'If your enemies are hungry, give them food to eat.'"

~Romans 12:17-21

Notes . . .

_____

_____

_____

_____

_____

Darren Hardy says that 2/3 of success and 4/5 of leadership is emotional competence. (If that is even half true, then we need to become more emotionally resilient.)

Where do we begin?

What if you took a one-year goal to work on *one* emotion. It took me a year to stop fighting with the people I love. It took me a year to have a respectful answer when they were grossly disrespectful. It took me a year to not let them push my buttons. It didn't mean they stopped pushing buttons, guilting me, manipulating . . . but I WASN'T DOING IT BACK! I stopped lecturing and started asking questions. I made it so much further working on ME than I ever did working on THEM!

We all want to grow our influence. This is the road to do it. Grow ourselves emotionally.

We are called to be extraordinary as leaders. Our emotions are lights on the dashboard to indicate something's wrong under the hood. If jealous or insecure or guilty, we need to look under the hood.

Emotions are simply dash board lights; not the steering wheel and there are four of them that can really take a leader out!

1. FEAR

-Fear triggers fight, flight or freeze. It can prevent you from taking a risk, having a tough conversation, holding someone accountable, or even being obedient to a prompt of God.

-What are the reasons you are afraid?

-Fear is just a roaring lion.

-Fear not, take heart.

For God did not give us a spirit of timidity or cowardice or fear, but [He has given us a spirit] of power and of love and of sound judgment and personal discipline [abilities that result in a calm, well-balanced mind and self-control]. (2 Timothy 1:7)

2. ANGER

-One ill-timed blow up can cost you much. A pattern of them can cost you your leadership.

-Patterns of angry blow ups need to be replaced with NEW patterns. You may need to get help with this. I did!

-Why are you angry? Even righteous anger is subject to self-control.

-Feel anger, but don't give it the steering wheel. Ephesians 4:26-27

Be angry and do not sin. Don't let the sun go down on your anger, and don't give the Devil an opportunity. (Ephesians 4:26-27)

3. DISCOURAGEMENT

-Discouragement is one of the top tactics used by the devil in order to take spiritual leaders out.

-Discouragement won't disqualify a leader like anger can. Won't shut you down completely shut down a leader like fear can. But it is enough to distract you from the mission by making you retreat within yourself.

-It is often based on a skewed truth or half-truth turned into a lie in your mind.

-To combat discouragement you must not isolate. Sometimes just saying it out loud is half the battle. Combat it with the truth!

-It doesn't hurt to allow others to encourage you! And you can always take David's advice!

4. INSECURITY

-Every woman has some insecurity. It can be minimal to debilitating.

-It can look like competition, comparison, shyness, caution, a façade.

-It is not one bomb that goes off, but many little fires that eventually burn down your leadership. It erodes trust and makes us SELF-CENTERED.

-Insecurity is an attack on our worth and value and is from the pit of Hell. It will become a thing of the past when we know what God says about our worth and how He values us and sees us.

FEAR

My sister dove in the water when my son eighteen-month-old jumped in the water. She saved my child. She said to me, *"What the hell is wrong with you?"* because I hadn't moved. I just stared in shock For YEARS, every time I made a motherly mistake, I heard those words. I FREEZE! I thought I was flawed. I realized this was my natural fear reaction. Not just for danger, but fear of failure, fear of rejection.

Last year, I wrote an email to myself. *"Maybe this is happening just so that you'll freeze because the enemy knows that's what you do and he doesn't want you to fulfill your destiny. So, maybe you need to intentionally not freeze."* This was a real thing. Fear prevents taking chances or even responding to God.

ANGER

I went to see somebody . . . a counselor. I went there to fix *my family*. Then, I realized it was I who needed the help.

She asked me questions and I would respond,"So-n-so di this and so I had to do this!

"Had to?"

"Well, it wasn't a gun to my head, but it was the only option?"

"The only option?"

I had lots of options, but I didn't like them. I deleted them. Now, I look at *all* my choices, even those I don't like. You may have to partner with somebody to overcome anger in your life. There's no shame in that. Lean on professionals, other friends. Don't look down on it or feel ashamed.

Read Ephesians 4:26-27. You CAN feel anger and not act on that. It's going to come on the dashboard of your life, but what will you do with that? If you understood you were giving the devil the opportunity when we act on anger, what choice would we make? Feel it, but don't give it the steering wheel.

DISCOURAGEMENT

Discouragement doesn't necessarily take a leader out, but it will slow you way down. And it's often based on a truth . . . that is skewed . . . basically, a lie.

Remember the truth:

Why, my soul, are you downcast? Why so disturbed within me? Put your hope in God, for I will yet praise him, my Savior and my God. (a Psalm 42:11 NIV)

So I say to my soul, "Don't be discouraged. Don't be disturbed. For I know my God will break through for me." Then I'll have plenty of reasons to praise him all over again. Yes, living before his face is my saving grace! (Psalm 42:11 TPT)

INSECURITY

Remember, the devil will use unsuspecting pawns for his purposes.

Search your Bibles. You will find that God sees us as:

o New (we have a new nature that actually can obey God!)

o Complete (all that was lacking was filled by Him) o Whole (It is finished)

o Healed (he no longer sees us as broken, or sick, needing a physician)

o Filled (when the Father looks at you, He sees Jesus)

o Washed (although we still "miss the mark" we are not sinners in His eyes)

o Forgiven (no score is being kept, He is not counting people's sins against them.)

o Worthy (because the price paid for us was Jesus' blood – an invaluable treasure)

o Daughters (we are adopted into His family)

o Royalty (and His family is ROYAL)

o Co-heirs with Jesus (since we are adopted; we get an equal piece of His "will")

o Sheep (He is the Good Shepherd and knows EXACLTY how much sheep need their shepherds)

o Called & Chosen (set apart for His purpose for your life – to glorify God and spread His Love and Light)

o Conquerors, overcomers, victors! (He knows how it ends.)

Spoiler Alert:

WE

WIN!

Forum Q2: Choose one of the 4 emotions that take us out and talk about how it has sabotaged your leadership in faith, family or business. Give us ONE tip for becoming resilient against it.

_____

_____

_____

_____

_____

From the Forum . . .

Anger

- You need to stop and breathe rather than react.
- PRAY.
- Ask what the RIGHT response is rather than the emotional response.
- Wait. Urgency is rooted in emotion.
- Is Anger unforgiveness? WHY are you angry? Can that be explained? Understanding doesn't necessarily mean agreement. Don't necessarily seek agreement; seek understanding.
- Is it justified anger or out-of-control emotion?
- Take space; if you can't walk away then take space internally. Close your eyes and take a deep breath. Anger wants to escalate, and it will if you allow it.
- Where there is anger there is no peace, it's interesting that God knew we needed Peace so importantly that

he made it part of the armor of God to protect our spirits. We have to always actively put on peace so we can go forward.

- Do not let the sun go down on your anger, and don't give the devil the opportunity.

Fear

- God has told us to Fear Not, so we know that it's not from him.
- Declare the truth!

Dicouragement

- Step back and press into the Lord and His Word. What does God's Word say about this?
- When I find myself in overwhelm in any life area, but often in business, I sense an inability to do ANY of it in my version of "good enough," so I shut down and do NONE of it, and instead find myself ruminating on all of the self-doubt. Thus, I end up even more overwhelmed and behind and get MORE discouraged. This discouragement pours out then in ALL areas of my life . . . faith, family, AND business. It pours out in a short temper and short fuse. It pours out in guilt and shame that I can't

"handle." All of these added emotions also add to overwhelm, but now it's both the real overwhelm of practical tasks and a mental and spiritual overwhelm. It's my own personal "ugly cycle." Pray truth into life to battle this emotion.

Insecurity

- Reprogram your mind and self-talk.
- (Romans 12:2)
- Affirmations (Consider making a voice memo on your phone and hear them back in your own voice.)
- Ask THINKING Questions. Human nature says that we're actually more likely to believe what comes out of our own mouths. The more you declare it, the more you begin to believe it.
- What God says about you is the truest thing about you. What God says overcomes your words, so why not make His words, yours?

There are three ways to handle your emotions and become more emotionally resilient:

1. Own your emotions
o No Blaming people (if someone can make you angry, does that mean they

can also make you happy, content, thankful?)
o No blaming circumstances (circumstances reveal our nature, they don't create it)
o Just own it (I feel blank about blank)
o If they are dashboard lights, what are they really indicating? Ask yourself:

o Am I really mad, or am I hurt, and have I had a conversation with God and the appropriate people?
o What am I really afraid about and what is God telling me to do?
o Why am I feeling insecure and what does God say about me?
o What is really discouraging me and what does God say about it?

2. Lead your emotions
o Although Emotional Dashboard lights can be blinding, YOU still hold the steering wheel in your hands (and you may need to pull this car over for a minute!)
o Self-control, an experiment o Self-control, a fruit of the Spirit and a worthy pursuit o Self-control, an anchor in the storms

3. Mature your emotions
o God's Word will mature you o Practice will mature you o Trials of

  various kinds will mature you o We
  think we can't until we have to

- (Lead your emotions) Imagine you're in your worst emotional moment and your pastor knocks on the door? What do you do? You reel it in. We do that when an important person walks in the room. Guess what? God is always in the room.
- (Mature) Your feelings aren't your God.
- I can do all things . . . I "CAN," instead of "I could never.

Today, I can do everything that is on my calendar. THAT needs to be one of my affirmations. Do it like we have to!

Forum Q3: What do you think it means to own your emotions, lead your emotions or mature your emotions.

_____

_____

_____

Closing Prayer . . .

Thank You so much for the women's forum. I'm grateful we can grow in You together. Put your hedge around us. We'll be tested in this area as women set out to grow, mature, become emotionally resilient We'll be tested through storms. I pray we can all rise and bring your remembrance to that. We are your hands created for good works. Our ability to fail does not overrule your ability to lift us up. We trust all this in Jesus Christ's name. Amen.

ACTION STEPS:

Find an accountability partner to help you reel in your emotional resilience and tap into God's gift of self-control.

Kimberly Joy Krueger and the Fellowship of Extraordinary Women

I believe women were created to be an answer for the problems our world faces today. The Fellowship of Extraordinary Women (FEW) was born out of that belief and today, FEW empowers women from all over the globe to live extraordinary lives and tell their stories.

FEW Monthly Meetings develop women's understanding of their true identity in Christ and empower them to embrace their God-given destiny. When I see women begin to understand that she was created to be an answer, she cannot help but to make a significant difference in the lives around her!

FEW's Certified Women's Leadership Course (CWLC) for Christian women changes the way they see God, themselves, and others. It catapults women into their God-given destiny as leaders on the seven mountains of cultural influence. I've experienced CWLC giving women unbridled confidence to be who God made them to be!

FEW International Publications, a #1 Bestselling Publisher with a unique writer-coaching model, is an extraordinary publishing experience. It is for women authors at all levels who are seeking more from telling their stories than just a printed project. I am privileged to watch authors connect, learn, and grow through the creation of a written work that impacts others and glorifies God.

Be Extraordinary!
Kimberly

Extraordinary Women; Extraordinary Stories
http://kimberlyjoykrueger.com/few.php

Made in the USA
Middletown, DE
08 July 2022